The Pursuit of Wisdom

DISCOVERY SERIES BIBLE STUDY
For individuals or groups

According to Alice Mathews, Proverbs 31 has been misunderstood, undervalued, and overlooked in what it contributes to our overall understanding of wisdom.

After reading this booklet, we may understand why Solomon wasn't the one to write the last chapter on wisdom. It is probably for good reason that this description was not written by a king who gave wisdom a bad name by collecting 700 wives and 300 concubines. As Alice and her co-writer Karen Mason show, the wisdom of King Lemuel, by contrast, describes Lady Wisdom in a way that will ennoble the life of any man or woman who honors her.

Alice and Karen do more than renew the vision of our need for wisdom. They also give us reason to remember that the wise sayings Solomon collected and spoke are neither a beginning nor an end in themselves. What could be more important than to rediscover wisdom's true source and how the book God inspired takes us beyond knowledge for the sake of knowledge!

—Mart DeHaan
Senior Advisor of Ministry Content
Our Daily Bread Ministries

This Discovery Series Bible Study is based on
The Call of Wisdom (HP132), one of the popular Discovery Series booklets from Our
Daily Bread Ministries. Find out more about Discovery Series at
discoveryseries.org

Discovery House is affiliated with Our Daily Bread Ministries,
Grand Rapids, Michigan.

Requests for permission to quote from this book should be directed to:
Permissions Department, Discovery House, PO Box 3566, Grand Rapids, MI 49501, or contact
us by e-mail at permissionsdept@dhp.org

Managing Editor: Dave Branon
Study Guide questions: Dave Branon
Graphic Design: Steve Gier

COVER PHOTO:
Public Domain Archive via Pixabay.com

INSIDE PHOTOS:
Arjun Kartha via FreeImages.com, p.6; Christophe Billard via Pixabay.com, p.9; Tabaluga via MorgueFile.com, p.10;
Evans888 via FreeImages.com, p.14; Lucas Cranach the Elder via Public Domain, p.16; Dantada via MorgueFile.com, p.17;
Taylorschlades via MorgueFile.com, p.22; Pinhed via MorgueFile.com, p.24; Wintersixfour via MorgueFile.com, p.25;
Thiago Felipe Festa via FreeImages.com, p.28; Hans Braxmeier via Pixabay.com, p.30; Blas Lamagni via FreeImages.com, p.31;
JackMoreh via FreeRangeStock.com, p.36; Manfred Antranias Zimmer via Pixabay.com, p.38.

ISBN: 978-1-62707-337-0
Printed in the United States of America
First Printing in 2015

Table of Contents

How To Use

DISCOVERY SERIES BIBLE STUDIES

The Purpose

The Discovery Series Bible Study (DSBS) series provides assistance to pastors and lay leaders in guiding and teaching fellow Christians with lessons adapted from Our Daily Bread Ministries Discovery Series booklets and supplemented with items taken from the pages of *Our Daily Bread*. The DSBS series uses the inductive study method to help Christians understand the Bible more clearly.

The Format

READ: Each DSBS book is divided into a series of lessons. For each lesson, you will read a few pages that will give you insight into one aspect of the overall study. Included in some studies will be FOCAL POINT and TIME OUT FOR THEOLOGY segments to help you think through the material. These can be used as discussion starters for group sessions.

RESPOND: At the end of the reading is a two-page STUDY GUIDE to help participants respond to and reflect on the subject. If you are the leader of a group study, ask each member to preview the STUDY GUIDE before the group gets together. Don't feel that you have to work your way through each question in the STUDY GUIDE; let the interest level of the participants dictate the flow of the discussion. The questions are designed for either group or individual study. Here are the parts of that guide:

MEMORY VERSE: A short Scripture passage that focuses your thinking on the biblical truth at hand and can be used for memorization. You might suggest memorization as a part of each meeting.

WARMING UP: A general interest question that can foster discussion (group) or contemplation (individual).

THINKING THROUGH: Questions that will help a group or a student interact with the reading. These questions help drive home the critical concepts of the book.

DIGGING IN: An inductive study of a related passage of Scripture, reminding the group or the student of the importance of Scripture as the final authority.

GOING FURTHER: A two-part wrap-up of the response: REFER suggests ways to compare the ideas of the lesson with teachings in other parts of the Bible. REFLECT challenges the group or the learner to apply the teaching in real life.

OUR DAILY BREAD: After each STUDY GUIDE session will be an *Our Daily Bread* article that relates to the topic. You can use this for further reflection or for an introduction to a time of prayer.

Go to the Leader's and User's Guide on page 39 for further suggestions about using this Discovery Series Bible Study.

INTRODUCTION:
The Call of Wisdom

saac Azimov was an American author and professor of biochemistry at Boston University. Authoring or editing more than 500 books, he observed, "The saddest aspect of life right now is that science gathers knowledge faster than society gathers wisdom." On another occasion he wrote, "Even as a youngster . . . I could not bring myself to believe that if knowledge presented danger, the solution was ignorance. To me, it always seemed that the solution had to be wisdom. You did not refuse to look at danger, rather you learned how to handle it safely."

What Asimov observed, we have lived. Who among us hasn't seen the pain brought by thoughtlessly speaking the truth without humility, love, or

■ FOCAL POINT

In the book of Psalms, wisdom is applied to things as they are and to prayer. The book of Proverbs applies wisdom to the practical relationships of life, and Ecclesiastes applies wisdom to the enjoyment of things as they actually are; there is no phase of life missed out, and it is shown that enjoyment is only possible by being related to God.

—OSWALD CHAMBERS
Shade of His Hand

wisdom? Who can estimate the costs of living in an age of science and technology without wisdom?

It seems noteworthy, therefore, that an institution as prestigious as the University of Chicago has initiated what it calls the Wisdom Research Project. An introduction of the effort explains: "Wisdom was once regarded as a subject worthy of rigorous scholarly inquiry in order to undertand its nature and benefits; however, until recently wisdom has been relatively overlooked as a topic for serious scholarly and scientific investigation. It is difficult to imagine a subject more central to the highest aspirations of being human."

In this lofty tribute to an ancient virtue, readers of the Bible might hear echoes of Solomon. *"Happy is the man who finds wisdom, and the man who gains understanding; for her proceeds are better than the profits of silver, and her gain than fine gold. She is more precious than rubies, and all the things you may desire cannot compare with her"* (PROVERBS 3:13–15).

In our day, Solomon is synonymous not only with wisdom but also with reckless self-absorption. Yet we do not dismiss the pursuit of wisdom, the first love of his life, as foolishness. Rather we long for the wisdom to end better than we have begun, to leave our world better than we found it, and to bring a smile to the face of others in the process.

Wisdom offers joy and satisfaction. According to the Bible, it is in wisdom that our Creator made the world, and then sacrificed himself to rescue it from the mess of our foolishness.

Such thoughts have given us a deep appreciation for the insights of Alice Mathews and Karen Mason on the last chapter of the Bible's most well-known book of wisdom. As we listen to them, we find fresh insight in the lauded and loathed "virtuous woman" of Proverbs 31. As they will explain in the chapters that follow, this section of Scripture has been misunderstood, undervalued, and overlooked in what it contributes to our overall understanding of wisdom.

By the time Alice and Karen are done, we may also understand why Solomon wasn't the one to write the last chapter on wisdom. It is probably for good reason that this description was not written by a king who gave wisdom a bad name by collecting 700 wives and 300 concubines. As Alice and Karen will show, the wisdom of King Lemuel, by contrast, describes Lady Wisdom in a way that ennobles the life of any man or woman who honors her.

> Wisdom offers joy and satisfaction. According to the Bible, it is in wisdom that our Creator made the world and then sacrificed himself to rescue us from the mess of our foolishness.

Alice and Karen do more than renew the vision of our need for wisdom. They give us reason to remember that the wise sayings Solomon collected and spoke are neither a beginning nor an end in themselves.

In a day when secular academia is remembering the lost art and treasure of wisdom, what could be more important than to rediscover wisdom's true source and how the book God inspired takes us beyond knowledge for the sake of knowledge!

—*Mart DeHaan*

INTRODUCTION:
The Call of Wisdom

MEMORY VERSE
Proverbs 3:13—

"Happy is the man who finds wisdom, and the man who gains understanding."

To be reminded of the importance of wisdom in an age of technology and science.

Warming Up

Where do you see wisdom displayed best these days? Give examples of those who have given wise counsel— and any specific wisdom they have shared.

First Thoughts

1. Mart DeHaan says, "Who among us hasn't seen the pain brought by thoughtlessly speaking the truth without humility, love, or wisdom" (pp. 6–7). When have you seen that played out in real life?

2. Solomon said, "Happy is the man who finds wisdom" (Proverbs 3:13). How does one go about finding wisdom?

3. What does Mart DeHaan mean by referring to the "virtuous woman" of Proverbs 31 as both "lauded and loathed"?

Getting Started

Research

Proverbs 31 is the inspired work of King Lemuel. Perhaps someone in the group can do some research to see who scholars think he is. Clearly, he is not one of the kings of Israel or Judah, so who is he?

1

The Strength to Be Wise

Certain passages in the Bible remind me of comedian Rodney Dangerfield's line: they "just don't get no respect." One of those texts is Proverb 31:10–31. Many men slide over this text because they're sure it's written only for women. Many women slide over it because they're sure it says something they don't want to hear. While most Christians know something about this passage, many choose to ignore it. But all of us—both men and women—need this important passage for three reasons. First and most basically, we need it because, under the inspiration of the Holy Spirit, it is included in the Bible. The apostle Paul reminded Timothy that all Scripture is given by inspiration of God and is profitable to us for doctrine, for reproof, for correction, and for instruction in righteousness. And that includes Proverbs 31.

Second, this passage lays out a summary of the wisdom of the people of God. The book of Proverbs opens by talking about the fear of the Lord as the beginning of knowledge (1:7), and it closes with praise for the person who fears the Lord (31:30). Chapter 1 introduces us to Lady Wisdom crying out in the streets of the city, calling young men to rethink their lives and their choices, and telling them to choose the fear of the Lord. Chapter 31 puts Lady Wisdom in street clothes, showing us what someone looks like who has wisely chosen to fear the Lord.

The third reason we need this important passage is the structure of the last twenty-two verses of the chapter itself. Proverbs 31:10–31 is an acrostic poem. Each verse of that section starts with a letter of the Hebrew alphabet (*aleph, beth, gimel, daleth, he, waw, etc.*). What's the point of that? In the ancient world, acrostics were used as memory devices. If you knew the letters of the alphabet, you could recall a series of ideas simply by recalling the next letter of the alphabet. We use memory devices today, but it was even more important in the an-

> Proverbs 31 summarizes the wisdom of God's people that is found throughout the book of Proverbs. It is for all of us to help us know how to live wisely.

cient world, in oral cultures in which the wisdom of a people was passed down from one generation to the next from mouth to ear. Children learned orally what they needed to know. An acrostic poem was one way to help them remember. Proverbs 31:10–31 was written as an acrostic poem so it could be memorized easily. It was meant to be learned by heart. Why? Because it summarizes the wisdom of God's people that is found throughout the book of Proverbs. It is for all of us to help us know how to live wisely.

The poem opens in verse 10 with a question and a statement: "A wife of noble character who can find? She is worth far more than rubies." That is how the New International Version of the Bible translates the Hebrew text. If you're reading in a New American Standard Bible, you'll find "An excellent wife, who can find?" But if you're reading in the New King James Version, it asks, "Who can find a virtuous wife?" When we see different translations of a Hebrew word that don't seem to mean exactly the same thing, we have to go back and ask how the Hebrew word was used in other parts of the Old Testament. This highly desirable woman, whose worth is far above rubies, is a *chayil* woman in Hebrew. In a sense, none of our translations—*noble character*, *excellent*, or *virtuous*—captures the feel of this Hebrew word. Chapter 31 has already used that Hebrew word in verses 2–3: "Listen, my son! Listen, son of my womb! Listen, my son, the answer to my prayers! Do not spend your strength (*chayil*) on women, your vigor on those who ruin kings" (NIV).

When we look at the usage of this Hebrew word throughout the Old Testament, we see that verse 3 more accurately translates it as *strength*.
It's a common word in the Bible, used 246 times. Three times it is used of a woman (Ruth 3:11, Proverbs 12:4, and here in Proverbs 31:10), but most often it describes soldiers or armies. The basic meaning of the word is "strength" or "power," and in the majority of cases it refers to military prowess. David's mighty men are *chayil* men.

● Focal Point

Strength and valor are not just masculine traits in the Bible. Many assert that the Bible teaches a man's identity is found in his strength and a woman's is found in her beauty. While this is true to a point, women as well as men are instructed to use their God-given strength for His purposes.

The use of the same word for *woman* or *wife* is common in both the Greek and Hebrew texts of Scripture. Context determines meaning of the word in a given passage.

The word is often translated as *valiant*, referring to a quality of valor needed in combat. A soldier stands firm in battle, refusing to desert his post or run away from duty. So a person who is *chayil* (like David's mighty men) has an inner strength to carry through on responsibilities and to overcome obstacles. Proverbs 31:10 is about this kind of person—strong, valiant, a person with inner strength who can overcome obstacles.

Some translations of verse 10 ask, "Who can find a virtuous *wife*?" the word translated *wife* is the same as for *woman*. Some translators have probably chosen the word *wife* because the next two verses talk about her husband. But this doesn't let single people off the hook! This strong, valiant person has wisdom or a skill for living, and in Proverbs 31 we see it personified in a wise woman. As we look at her, we see what wisdom looks like in daily life. The qualities of this woman are qualities that summarize the wisdom of the people of God. They are qualities for singles as well as married, for men as well as for women.

> A person who is **CHAYIL** (like David's mighty men) has inner strength to carry through on responsibilities and to overcome obstacles.

The Strength to Be Wise

To begin to understand in a fresh way why Proverbs 31 is important to men *and* women.

MEMORY VERSE
Proverbs 31:10—

"Who can find a virtuous wife? For her worth is far above rubies."

Warming Up

Having heard many messages on Proverbs 31 over the years, most Christians have an idea what it is saying. What are the most common concepts presented in this passage?

Thinking Through

1. The authors say, "Many women slide over [Proverbs 31:10–31] because they're sure it says something they don't want to hear" (p. 10). What do you think they are alluding to regarding women and Proverbs 31?

2. One of the key words in this passage is "strength." The Hebrew word *chayil* is used in verse 2 regarding men and in verse 10 regarding women ("virtuous"). What is the significance of this?

3. The word for "wife" in 31:10 can be translated "woman." What difference does this make, according to the authors?

Going Further

Refer

Look at each of these verses, and examine how *chayil* is used to describe these people:
Joshua 10:7: "warriors"

Judges 6:12: "warrior"

Ruth 3:11: "woman"

1. Discuss the significance that King Lemuel's words, which are a part of the inspired Scripture, seem also to have been inspired by his mother.

1 The words of King Lemuel, the utterance which his mother taught him:

2 What, my son! And what, son of my womb? And what, son of my vows?

3 Do not give your strength to women, nor your ways to that which destroys kings.

2. What do you make of verse 3, in which King Lemuel says, "Do not give your strength to women"?

8 Open your mouth for the speechless, in the cause of all who are appointed to die.

9 Open your mouth, judge righteously, and plead the cause of the poor and needy.

10 Who can find a virtuous wife? For her worth is far above rubies.

3. How can we incorporate King Lemuel's teaching in verses 8 and 9 into our lives?

Prayer Time ➤

Use the *Our Daily Bread* article on the next page as a guide for a devotional time about wisdom.

Reflect

What are you expecting to glean from a study of Proverbs 31?

What are some common teachings that you have heard from Proverbs 31 in the past? Keep those in mind, and revisit this question once the study is complete.

A Woman of Influence

Portraits of Martin Luther and his wife, **Katharina Von Bora** by Lucas Cranach the Elder.

During the early years of the Protestant Reformation in Europe, Katharina Von Bora, a former nun, married Martin Luther (1525). By all accounts, the two had a joyous married life. Luther said, "There is no bond on earth so sweet, nor any separation so bitter, as that which occurs in a good marriage."

Because Katharina rose at 4 a.m. to care for her responsibilities, Luther referred to her as the "morning star of Wittenberg." She was industrious in tending the vegetable garden and orchard. Also, she administered the family business and managed the Luthers' home and property. In time, the couple had six children for whom Katharina felt the home was a school of character development. Her energetic industry and care for the family made her a woman of influence.

Katharina seems to have been a woman like the one described in Proverbs 31. She was indeed a virtuous wife who awoke "while it [was] yet night" and provided "food for her household" (v. 15). She also watched "over the ways of her household, and [did] not eat the bread of idleness" (v. 27).

From role models like Katharina, we can learn about the love, diligence, and fear of the Lord that's needed to be a woman of influence.

—*Dennis Fisher*

PROVERBS
31:27—

She watches over the ways of her household, and does not eat eat the bread of idleness.

■ Read today's *Our Daily Bread* at **odb.org**

16

2

Wisdom Personified

So what characterizes a person of strength? The first characteristic of a wise woman is that she is *trustworthy*.

In verses 11 and 12 we read: "Her husband has full confidence in her and lacks nothing of value. She brings him good, not harm, all the days of her life" (NIV). It's clear that this woman's husband can trust her, knowing she won't blow the budget or run off with the mailman. She is trustworthy.

Are you a trustworthy person? Can you be trusted to do good, not harm, all the days of your life? If so, you are on your way to being a full-fledged Proverbs 31 wise person of strength.

In verses 13 through 18 we discover that this valiant, strong, committed, wise person is also *shrewd*. Most of us don't like the sound of that word, but the dictionary tells us that it simply means someone who is intelligent or clever. A shrewd person is not someone who takes advantage of other *people* but who takes advantage of *opportunities*. This is what shrewdness looks like in verses 13 through 18: Verse 13 states that the wise, strong woman "seeks wool and flax, and willingly works with her hands." She doesn't grab just anything that is handy but chooses her tasks and her materials with care.

Verses 14 and 15 liken this wise, strong woman to "merchant ships" bringing her "food from afar." She gets up while it is still dark and "provides food for her household" and "for her maidservants." This wise woman looks ahead and prepares for the future, not just for the present. She goes about her work so that everyone in her household has what they need.

Verse 16 shows us this woman's acumen: "She considers a field and buys it; from her profits she plants a vineyard." She is shrewd about purchasing property, and then she sets about making it produce a profit. She thinks through her projects carefully and plans how to carry them out successfully.

Verse 17 tells us that "she sets about her work vigorously; her arms are strong for her tasks" (NIV). The Hebrew actually means that she makes her arms strong for her task so she can do her work with vigor. The shrewd person improves her knowledge and skill in order to work smarter, not harder.

Verse 18 is clear that "she sees that her trading is profitable, and her lamp does not go out at night" (NIV). This wise woman makes quality products that she can sell to the merchants without shame or fear.

■ Focal Point

The strong and wise woman is trustworthy, not just trusted. Her husband's trust is well placed because of her character. By implication, all who deal with this strong, wise woman can also trust her because she is worthy of their confidence just as she is worthy of her husband's.

In short, a *chayil* person is shrewd. So ask yourself: How shrewd am I in my daily activities? Do I think through my projects so I can carry them out successfully? Do I plan ahead? Do I commit myself to do good work? If you can answer yes to these questions, you have the second characteristic of wisdom in the book of Proverbs. You are shrewd or intelligent or wise.

In verses 19 and 20 we move to the third characteristic of a *chayil* person: "In her hand she holds the distaff and grasps the spindle with her fingers. She opens her arms to the poor and extends her hands to the needy" (NIV). The third characteristic of a wise person is *generosity*. That may not be immediately obvious in the text because our English translations do not catch the link between verse 19 and verse 20. But in the Hebrew the two verses cannot be separated for this reason: the first half of 19 and the last half of verse 20 have the same grammatical structure and the same verb; the same is true for the last half of verse 19 and the first part of verse 20—the same structure and the same verb. When that happens, we have what is called a *chiasm* (which looks like a big X). The wise woman spun thread and wove sashes and made garments to sell to merchants *so* she could be generous to the poor and needy. Shrewdness must always be tempered by generosity. Otherwise it becomes greed. And the Bible doesn't say nice things about greedy people. So a shrewd person takes advantage of opportunities in order to have something to give to those in need.

> Ask yourself: How shrewd am I in my daily activities? Do I think through my projects so that I can carry them out successfully? Do I plan ahead? Do I commit myself to do good work? If you can answer yes to these questions, you have the second characteristic of wisdom in the book of Proverbs. You are shrewd or intelligent or wise.

The fourth characteristic of a *chayil* person is found in the next five verses (21–25), showing us that a wise person is also *diligent*: Verse 21 states that "when it snows, she has no fear for her household; for all of them are clothed in scarlet" (NIV). How often does it snow in the Middle East? Not that often. But when it does snow, this diligent, wise woman has made provision for her household. The translation of the final word in that verse is a bit amusing. Apparently the Hebrew word translated *scarlet* can also be translated *lined garments*. If it's snowing outside, I am more interested in wearing clothing with linings that keep me warm than something that is merely red in color.

Verse 22 tells us that "she makes coverings for her bed; she is clothed in fine linen and purple" (NIV). "Fine linen and purple" attests to the fact that this woman is diligent in caring for her own needs as well as the needs of others. She dresses well.

Verse 23 connects her diligence to her husband's position in the community: "Her husband is respected at the city gate [the community center], where

■ Focal Points

- The wise and strong person has learned to hold what they have with open hands. They are thankful for it, but they are not defined by it.
- A shrewd person takes advantage of opportunities in order to have something to give to those in need.

he takes his seat among the elders of the land" (NIV). This wise woman's handling of life earns respect for her husband from the leaders of the community.

Verse 24 explains some specifics of this wise woman's earning power: "She makes linen garments and sells them, and supplies the merchants with sashes" (NIV). Her work with distaff and spindle isn't merely a hobby; it is a means of producing income for her family in order to help those who are in need.

As a result, verse 25 concludes that "she is clothed [not just in fine linen

■ Focal Point

The Hebrew word for *strength* in verse 25 is **oz**. It means "strength, might, and power." It is often used to describe fortresses.

and purple but] with strength and dignity; she can laugh at the days to come" (NIV). Some people dismiss diligence as workaholism or obsessive-compulsiveness. But diligence is a necessary part of wisdom.

Verse 26 gives us the fifth characteristic of a wise person: "She speaks with wisdom, and faithful instruction is on her tongue" (NIV). The strong, wise person always speaks wisely and kindly. A wise person not only walks the walk but she also talks the talk.

Wisdom Personified

STUDY GUIDE 2
read pages 17–21

To examine the characteristics of a godly person of strength.

MEMORY VERSE
Proverbs 31:26—

"She opens her mouth with wisdom, and on her tongue is the law of kindness."

Warming Up

As you think about the people you know best, who are some people who demonstrate true strength—strength of character and strength to handle life's difficulties? What can you learn from those people?

Thinking Through

1. The authors lead off this chapter with a tough question: "Are you a trustworthy person?" What are some traits that help you know if you are trustworthy or not? What leads you to call someone else trustworthy?

2. Notice what the authors said about the word *shrewd*. What are some good characteristics of being shrewd, according to Proverbs 31:13–18?

3. We are all known by how we talk to others. Flesh out what the authors mean at the end of the chapter when they say, "A wise person not only walks the walk but she also talks the talk."

Going Further

Refer

In verse 17, the woman "sets about her work vigorously" (NIV). What can you learn about the word *vigorously* by looking at these verses, which also have the Hebrew word *oz*, which means "might or strength"?

2 Samuel 6:14: "David danced before the Lord with all his *might*."

Psalm 28:7: "The LORD is my *strength* and my shield."

Psalm 84:5: "Blessed is the man whose *strength* is in [God]."

1. Proverbs 31 gives us a great picture of a man and wife working as a team. How do we see this from verses 11–12, 16, 23, 26? What does this successful team look like?

2. At the same time, we can see that a *chayil* woman could be single. If she is, what are some powerful characteristics she should have that will help her in life to be a godly woman? See verses 14, 18, 20, 24–26.

3. What does it mean that this person of Proverbs 31 is clothed with "strength and honor" (v. 25)? And how can that bring future rejoicing?

¹¹ The heart of her husband safely trusts her; so he will have no lack of gain.

¹² She does him good and not evil all the days of her life.

¹³ She seeks wool and flax, and willingly works with her hands.

¹⁴ She is like the merchant ships, she brings her food from afar. ¹⁵ She also rises while it is yet night, and provides food for her household, and a portion for her maidservants.

¹⁶ She considers a field and buys it; from her profits she plants a vineyard.

¹⁷ She girds herself with strength, and strengthens her arms.

¹⁸ She perceives that her merchandise is good, and her lamp does not go out by night…

²⁰ She extends her hand to the poor,…

²¹ She is not afraid of snow for her household, for all her household is clothed with scarlet.

²² She makes tapestry for herself; her clothing is fine linen and purple.

²³ Her husband is known in the gates, when he sits among the elders of the land.

²⁴ She makes linen garments and sells them, and supplies sashes for the merchants.

²⁵ Strength and honor are her clothing; she shall rejoice in time to come.

²⁶ She opens her mouth with wisdom, and on her tongue is the law of kindness.

Prayer Time

Use the *Our Daily Bread* article on the next page as a guide for a devotional time about wisdom.

Reflect

Three words that stand out from this section are *trustworthy, shrewd,* and *wise.* What has this section taught you about those three terms? What kinds of changes do you see yourself making to incorporate those ideas more completely in your life?

A Helping Hand

In the 1930s, jockey Johnny Longden was rammed in mid-race. While thundering steeds came up from behind, Johnny was thrown sideways off his horse. Seeing his predicament, another jockey reached out and attempted to push Longden back up on his mount. Unfortunately, he pushed too hard and Longden flew over the horse onto the other side. Still another jockey nearby grabbed him and was able to help him safely back on his horse. Amazingly, Johnny Longden won the race! A newspaper dubbed it "the ultimate impossibility." Helping hands had not only saved him from severe injury and possible death, but allowed him to win the race.

As believers, we are to offer a helping hand to others as well. In Proverbs 31, we read of the virtuous woman who "extends her hand to the poor, yes, she reaches out her hands to the needy" (v. 20). For centuries, the compassion of this woman of faith has been an inspiration to both men and women. She helps to remind us that extending ourselves to others is a biblical virtue to be exhibited by all believers.

There are many who are struggling or have fallen on hard times and need our assistance. Who in your life needs a helping hand?

—*Dennis Fisher*

PROVERBS 31:20—

She extends her hand to the poor, yes, she reaches out her hands to the needy.

■ Read today's *Our Daily Bread* at **odb.org**

The Proper
Perspective
PART 1

At this point you may be thinking that being wise or strong or valiant is too much work. It's too demanding! Does it really matter that I'm dependable and thoughtful about my work? Or that I'm generous and diligent in all that I do? Or that I watch my tongue and use it wisely? Wisdom, as described throughout the book of Proverbs, is about making wise decisions in the thick of life. And in Proverbs 8:35–36 Lady Wisdom tells us that those who love her will live, but those who sin against her will wrong their own souls. Wisdom is the stuff of everyday life, but it is also the stuff of life and death.

But Proverbs 31 doesn't end with verse 26. If it did, we would have a moral code but no resource beyond our own determination to make it work. What *makes* us wise isn't found in verses 11 through 26. It is found in verse 30: "Charm is deceptive, and beauty is fleeting; but a woman who fears the LORD is to be praised" (NIV). Here's the bottom line: the wise person, the strong, committed person, *knows the difference between what passes and what lasts. The wise person chooses to live for what is eternal.* Verse 30 tells us that charm is deceitful and beauty is fleeting. Beauty is good, but it doesn't last. What lasts forever is our relationship with God.

Sermons I've heard on Proverbs 31 have tended to focus on the woman's skills, her busyness. These are *evidences* of wisdom, but they are not the point of the passage. True wisdom starts with God and our relationship with Him. It starts with "the fear of the Lord." What is this "fear" of God? Is it terror in God's presence? No, it is a reverent understanding of who God is and where we stand in relationship to Him. The single most important thing that you and I can know is who God is. We must know Him as our Creator, our Redeemer, and our Sustainer.

We must know that God is our Creator. The psalmist captured this:

> *You created my inmost being; you knit me together in my mother's womb. I praise you because I am fearfully and wonderfully made; your works are wonderful, I know that full well. My frame was not hidden from you when I was made in the secret place, when I was woven together in the depths of the earth.* (PSALM 139:13–15 NIV).

We do not draw our next breath unless God our Creator enables us. The apostle Paul told the Athenians that it is in God that we live and move and have our being (ACTS 17:25–28).

We must know that God is our Redeemer. Again David the psalmist gave voice to this for us:

Praise the LORD, my soul, and forget not all his benefits—who forgives all your sins and heals all your diseases, who redeems your life from the pit and crowns you with love and compassion, who satisfies your desires with good things so that your youth is renewed like the eagle's (PSALM 103:2–5 NIV).

Through faith in Jesus Christ our Redeemer we have new life. He has taken the punishment for our sins and has redeemed us (or bought us back) from Satan for God. We must know that God is our Redeemer.

We also must know that God is our Sustainer. The Old Testament prophet Isaiah put it this way.

> We must know that God is our Redeemer. In the routine of daily life on in the crises that overtake us, God is our Sustainer.

Do you not know? Have you not heard? The LORD is the everlasting God, the Creator of the ends of the earth. He will not grow tired or weary, and his understanding no one can fathom. He gives strength to the weary and increases the power of the weak. Even youths grow tired and weary, and young men stumble and fall; but those who hope in the LORD will renew their strength. They will soar on wings like eagles; they will run and not grow weary, they will walk and not be faint (ISAIAH 40:28–31 NIV).

In the routine of daily life or in the crises that overtake us, God is our Sustainer.

3

The Proper Perspective (PART 1)

STUDY GUIDE
read pages 25–27

MEMORY VERSE
Proverbs 31:30—
"A woman who fears
the LORD, she shall be
praised."

To begin to understand that wisdom means having an eternal perspective

Warming Up

What are some things in this life that we put a lot of emphasis on but that are really fleeting? Why do we pay so much attention to those kinds of things?

Thinking Through

1. The authors say, "Wisdom is the stuff of everyday life, but it is also the stuff of life and death" (p. 26). What do you think that means in connection with Proverbs 8:35–36?

2. The authors define "the fear of the Lord" as "a reverent understanding of who God is and where we stand in relationship to Him" (p. 26). How does that definition help you in understanding Proverbs 31:30?

3. To understand a true relationship with God, it's important to know that He is our Sustainer. How does Isaiah 40:28–31 clarify that for us?

Going Further

Refer

These verses help us as we seek to know God as Creator, Redeemer, and Sustainer. What do they teach us?

Ecclesiastes 12:1

Job 19:25

Nehemiah 9:21

1. Verse 27 says that the woman being discussed in this chapter "does not eat the bread of idleness." What principles for parents can come from that simple phrase?

27 She watches over the ways of her household, and does not eat the bread of idleness.
28 Her children rise up and call her blessed; her husband also, and he praises her:
29 "Many daughters have done well, but you excel them all."
30 Charm is deceitful and beauty is passing, but a woman who fears the LORD, she shall be praised.
31 Give her of the fruit of her hands, and let her own works praise her in the gates."

2. In what ways is charm deceitful and beauty passing (v. 30)? What does that tell us about the truly important things in life?

3. How important is it for all of us to let our "own works" praise us instead of seeking the approval of people?

Prayer Time ➤

Use the *Our Daily Bread* article on the next page as a guide for a devotional time about wisdom.

Reflect

The authors suggest that the person singled out in Proverbs 31 can do the great things he or she does because those actions are evidences of a relationship with God. What are some ways to enhance that personal connection with our great Creator, Redeemer, and Sustainer?

Authentic Beauty

I often take a moment as I wait at our grocery store check-out stand to scan the covers of the magazines displayed there. It seems that if they aren't about sex and money, they're about diet, fitness, health, and outward beauty. There's nothing there for the soul.

The problem is that people read the wrong magazines—those that are full of lies that fixate on beauty of face and form as though that's all there is. This can lead to comparison and terrible despair.

Some years ago, a friend of mine told of a conversation he had with a lovely, self-assured teenager. "You're very self-confident," he observed. "Can you tell me why?" "Yes," the young woman answered. "It's because I'm so pretty." "Oh, I'm sorry," he said with extraordinary wisdom. "Why?" she asked in surprise. "Because," he replied, "you may not always be pretty."

"Charm is deceitful and beauty is passing" is the wisdom we read in Proverbs 31. Physical beauty all too quickly fades away; all one's efforts to keep it are doomed to fail. But there is an inner beauty—authentic beauty that will endure forever—in the one "who fears the LORD" (v. 30).

—*David Roper*

PROVERBS 31:30—
Charm is deceitful and beauty is passing, but a woman who fears the LORD, she shall be praised.

■ Read today's *Our Daily Bread* at **odb.org**

4

The Proper Perspective

PART 2

At **4:30 one Saturday morning** in 1994 our phone rang, waking my husband and me (Alice). Such a call is most likely bad news, a prank call, or a drunk calling a wrong number.

For us, it was bad news.

On the other end of the line was our oldest daughter, Susan, calling from the south of France where she and her family lived. She had just received a call from the ministry in the north of France where Kent, our only son, worked with profoundly disabled adults. Kent, on his way to a meeting while riding his bicycle, had been struck and killed by a drunk driver.

At a time like that people ask all kinds of questions.

- *Is God sovereign—could He have kept it from happening?*
- *Is God love?*
- *Does God care?*
- *Is God there?*

It is in the face of a tragedy and in the midst of sorrow that somehow we must grasp the cord of truth about God revealed in Scripture: God *is* sovereign and in some way works through tragedy. God *is* love in ways that we may not grasp in this life but one day will be plain to us. God *does* care and will use this for good in our lives. God *is* there. He is with us.

The writer of the letter to the Hebrews reminds us that God never leaves us nor forsakes us in the worst of times when our fears and tears threaten to overwhelm us (HEBREWS 13:5, quoting DEUTERONOMY 31:6).

This awareness of God at work even in tragedy gives us a different way to see life and see pain. *Knowing God* sustains us in our darkest moments and teaches us the difference between what passes and what lasts. But *knowing God* also sustains us in daily life.

> It is in the face of tragedy
> and in the midst of sorrow that somehow
> we must grasp the cord of truth about God
> revealed in Scripture:
> God is sovereign and in some way works
> through tragedy.

> In times of trouble, we find that
> our only fortress is the Lord.
> "Lord, my strength and my fortress,
> my refuge in times of distress,
> to you the nations will come from the
> ends of the earth and say, 'Our ancestors
> possessed nothing but false gods,
> worthless idols that did them
> no good.' "
>
> JEREMIAH 16:19 (NIV)

- It's not easy to be trustworthy, but God is there and sees that we can be trusted.
- It's not convenient to be shrewd, but God sees our work and is honored by it.
- It's not easy to be generous, but God cares about our generosity.
- It's not fun to be diligent, but we work to glorify God our Maker.
- It's not easy to speak wisely and kindly all the time, but God hears what we say.

Our relationship with God gives us a different perspective on life. We know what matters. We know what lasts and what passes away, and we choose what lasts eternally. And we bring that perspective to every choice we make—whether or not to be trustworthy, whether or not to plan ahead and work with care, whether or not to show compassion, whether or not to pursue our goals with diligence, whether or not to control our tongues. What we believe about God determines how wisely we live.

The fear or reverent awe of God motivates us to manage our time wisely

> # The remarkable thing about fearing God is that when you fear God you fear nothing else.
>
> ## OSWALD CHAMBERS

in the light of eternal values. The fear of the Lord motivates us to use our resources wisely to benefit others. The fear of the Lord helps us evaluate every choice we make each day.

A hundred years ago Ella Wheeler Wilcox, who is most famous for her line, "Laugh, and the world laughs with you; weep, and you weep alone," published a short poem whose lines are as true today as they were a century ago when she wrote them:

> *One ship sails East,*
> *And another West,*
> *By the self-same winds that blow;*
> *'Tis the set of sails*
> *And not the gales,*
> *That tells the way we go.*

It's the set of the sail and not the gale. It's your choice. Men and women, singles and marrieds, learn from Proverbs 31. Choose to live wisely in the light of what lasts forever. If you do, you will be characterized by a strong commitment, by trustworthiness, by shrewdness, by generosity, by diligence, and by a controlled tongue.

Even more, you'll know the difference between what passes and what lasts—and you'll give yourself to what lasts for eternity. That's God's formula for living life with skill. Be wise. Be a person of strength.

It's your choice.

■ Focal Point

Every now and again when you look at life from a certain angle it seems as if evil and wrong . . . are having it all their own way and you feel that everything must go to pieces; but it doesn't; around it is the sovereignty of God.

Oswald Chambers
God's Workmanship

The Proper Perspective (PART 2)

STUDY GUIDE
read pages 31–35

To see how the sustaining power of God helps us in the face of tragedy.

MEMORY VERSE
Hebrews 13:5—

"For [God] Himself has said, 'I will never leave you nor forsake you.' "

Warming Up

What is the worst tragedy you have had to endure in your life? Was there any point at which you had to remind yourself that God is in control and could take care of you?

Thinking Through

1. The unthinkable happened to Alice Mathews and her husband. They lost their son in a biking accident. What were the key questions she said they grappled with upon hearing about Kent's death? What other questions do you think would come to mind?

2. Alice said, "*Knowing God* sustains us in our darkest moments and teaches us the difference between what passes and what lasts" (p. 32). What do you think she meant by that statement?

3. How does "the fear of the Lord" help us "evaluate every choice we make each day" (p. 34)?

Going Further

Refer

Discuss the implications of the following verses as they relate to the idea of God and His ability to do the miraculous.

Job 38:4–7

Job 40:2

Job 42:2

1. What a promise we have in verse 19! What comfort is found in verse 19 for one who is in the midst of "the day of affliction"?

2. How do we handle life when someone lies about the truth of God's presence in our life?

3. How does God give us assurance of hope in time of trouble, according to verse 21?

[19] O LORD, my strength and my fortress, my refuge in the day of affliction, the Gentiles shall come to You from the ends of the earth and say, "Surely our fathers have inherited lies, worthlessness and unprofitable things." [20] Will a man make gods for himself, which are not gods?

[21] "Therefore behold, I will this once cause them to know, I will cause them to know My hand and My might; And they shall know that My name is the Lord.

Prayer Time ➤

Use the *Our Daily Bread* article on the next page as a guide for a devotional time about wisdom.

Reflect

Is it possible to prepare yourself ahead of time for a possible tragedy in life? What are specifics, according to the authors in this section?

God's Astonishing Promise

The writer to the Hebrews quotes God as saying to His people, "I will never leave you nor forsake you" (Hebrews 13:5). How does that strike you? Is it just some pleasant piety that evokes a wide yawn?

This isn't like saying we have coffee with the President or a Supreme Court justice. Knowing people like that would say something significant about us. But to claim that God is with us every moment of every day, as close as our skin, in every turn of life, tear-stained or drenched in smiles—some would say that borders on insanity.

Yet throughout history men and women have staked their lives on that truth. Abraham, Moses, Rahab, Joshua, David, Esther, just to name a few. The promise was true for them, but how can we know it's true for us?

It is true for us because of Jesus. By His coming, He says, "I want to be with you; I gave myself to you; I gave myself for you. Do you really think I would ever forsake you?"

How do you respond to this astonishing promise? Say it's too good to be true. Say it sounds unbelievable. But don't ignore it. In your hurts, your fears, your struggles, your temptations, there is no more wonderful promise than this: "I will never leave you nor forsake you."

—Haddon Robinson

Hebrews 13:5—
[God] Himself has said, "I will never leave you nor forsake you."

■ Read today's
Our Daily Bread at
odb.org

■ LEADER'S and USER'S GUIDE

Overview of Lessons: Beyond Reasonable Doubt

Pulpit Sermon Series (for pastors and church leaders)

Although the Discovery Series Bible Study is primarily for personal and group study, pastors may want to use this material as the foundation for a series of messages on this important issue. The suggested topics and their corresponding texts from the Overview of Lessons above can be used as an outline for a sermon series.

DSBS User's Guide (for individuals and small groups)

Individuals—Personal Study
• Read the designated pages of the book.
• Carefully consider the study questions, and write out answers for each.

Small Groups—Bible-Study Discussion
• To maximize the value of the time spent together, each member should do the lesson work prior to the group meeting.
• Recommended discussion time: 45 minutes.
• Engage the group in a discussion of the questions—seeking full participation from each member.